D1272889

SAVING WILDLIFE

Polar Animals

by Sonya Newland

A+
Smart Apple Media

Published by Smart Apple Media
P.O. Box 3263, Mankato, Minnesota 56002

Printed in the United States of America at Corporate Graphics,
in North Mankato, Minnesota.

Published by arrangement with the
Watts Publishing Group Ltd., London.

Library of Congress Cataloging-in-Publication Data
Newland, Sonya.
Polar animals / by Sonya Newland.
p. cm. -- (Saving wildlife)
Includes bibliographical references and index.
Summary: "Presents endangered species of the North and South pole ecosystems, discusses the harmful effects global warming and human activities have on them, and introduces conservation efforts. Includes maps, diagrams, reading quiz, and ways readers can contribute"--Provided by publisher.
ISBN 978-1-59920-659-2 (library binding)
1. Animals--Polar regions--Juvenile literature. 2. Wildlife conservation--Juvenile literature. I. Title.
QL104.N49 2012
591.70911--dc22

2010026854

Produced for Franklin Watts by
White-Thomson Publishing
Series consultant: Sally Morgan
Designer: Tim Mayer
Picture researcher: Amy Sparks

Picture Credits
Dreamstime: 9b (Bobby17), 18 (Carrieanne), 27t (2pley); **Nature Picture Library:** 6 (Martha Holmes), 17t (Doug Allan), 17b (Martha Holmes), 25t (Doc White); **Photolibrary:** Cover (Gavriel Jecan), 5 (Tips Italia), 8 (Splashdown Direct), 13t (Tom Ulrich), 14 (Wayne Lynch), 19 (Jo Overholt), 21b (Doug Allan), 24 (Jo Overholt); **Shutterstock:** 4 (Galina Barskaya), 7 (Andy38), 9t (Jean-Pierre Lavoie), 10 (Ron Hilton), 11t (JG Photo), 11b (Denis Pepin), 12t (Nadezhda Bolotina), 12b (Mayskyphoto), 13b (Chris Alcock), 15t (Geoffrey Kuchera), 15b (Morten Hilmer), 16 (Darren Begley), 20 (Gentoo Multimedia Ltd.), 21t (Photodynamic), 22 (Sandy Maya Matzen), 23t (Daniel Hebert), 23m (nice_pictures), 23b (Paula Cobleigh), 25b (Albert H. Teich), 26b (Johann Helgason); **Wikimedia:** 27b.

1019
3-2011

9 8 7 6 5 4 3 2 1

Contents

Words in **bold** are in the glossary on page 31.

Polar Habitats

The polar regions surround the North and South poles at the very top and bottom of our planet. These frozen areas are the harshest environments on earth.

The Arctic

The Arctic is the region that lies within the Arctic Circle, an imaginary line around earth close to the North Pole. To the south of the Arctic Ocean is an area called the **tundra**. The land is always frozen here. South of the tundra is a cold forest area known as the **taiga**, where bears, deer, and many small animals live.

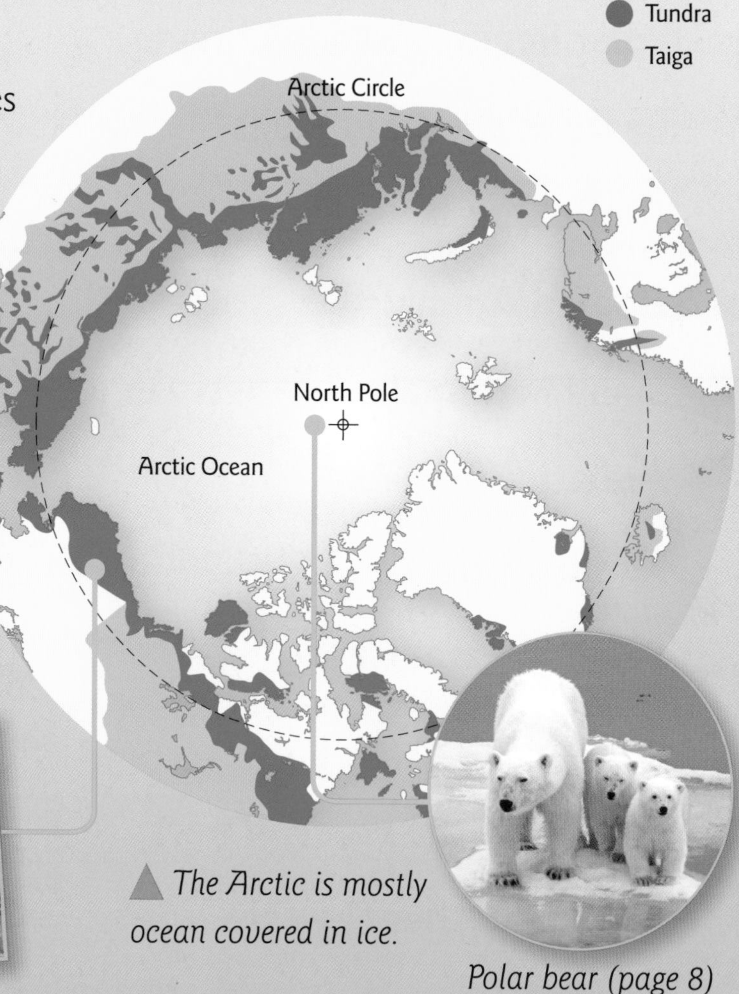

▲ *The Arctic is mostly ocean covered in ice.*

Polar bear (page 8)

Caribou (page 12)

EXTREME ANIMALS

Elephant seals of the Antarctic are the largest seals in the world. Adult males can weigh more than a car!

Emperor penguin (page 20)

Humpback whale (page 24)

Leopard seal (page 16)

*Antarctica is a whole **continent** surrounded by the Southern Ocean.*

The Antarctic

Within the Antarctic Circle, close to the South Pole, lies Antarctica, the coldest continent on earth. There are almost no living creatures on the land there, but the Southern Ocean that surrounds Antarctica is teeming with life.

Life at the Poles

It is so cold at the poles that both land and sea are frozen for most of the year. This makes it hard for anything to live there, but some creatures have **adapted** to life in these tough conditions. They often have white coats so they blend in with their snowy **habitat**, and thick layers of body fat keep them warm. Some humans even live in the Arctic, including the Inuit people, who survive by fishing and hunting Arctic animals.

*The **Inuit** build temporary homes called igloos out of snow when they are on hunting trips.*

Polar Regions under Threat

Once, the biggest threat to polar animals was hunting by humans—for their fur, fat, or just for sport. Hunting is still a danger, but now there are other factors affecting the animals' chances of survival.

Melting Ice

Global warming is having a more dramatic effect at the poles than anywhere else on earth. As it gets warmer, the ice melts, so animals have to survive on smaller areas of land. As the polar oceans warm up, some fish and other sea creatures die out. This affects animals further up the **food chain**, which rely on them as a source of food.

▲ *All polar animals rely on others for their food. This leopard seal in Antarctica is eating an emperor penguin.*

Human Activity

Humans are settling in areas where animals had previously lived undisturbed. Experts also believe there is oil beneath the Arctic ice. Drilling for oil disturbs **native** animals and can cause **pollution**.

Saving Polar Animals

Over thousands of years, the animals that live in polar regions have adapted to their environment. They will not survive if changes to their habitat continue. If people do not work to save them, many **species** will be lost.

WHAT DO YOU THINK?

Searching for oil in the Arctic could provide humans with an important **resource**, but some experts are worried that it would scare away the animals and cause pollution. What ways might there be of meeting the needs of humans while protecting wildlife?

▼ *Humans are settling in what were once uninhabited polar regions. This is Murmansk, the largest town within the Arctic Circle.*

ENDANGERED ANIMALS

The International Union for Conservation of Nature (IUCN, see page 28) lists animals according to how **endangered** they are.

Extinct: Died out completely
Extinct in the wild: Only survive in captivity
Critically endangered: Extremely high risk of becoming **extinct** in the near future
Endangered: High risk of becoming extinct in the wild
Vulnerable: High risk of becoming endangered in the wild
Near threatened: Likely to become endangered in the near future
Least concern: Lowest risk of becoming endangered

Bears of the Cold Poles

Polar bears have become a symbol of the Arctic, but they are not the only big bears that roam the frozen landscape of the Far North.

White Bears

Polar bears live on the land and sea ice of the Arctic. Beneath their white fur, their skin is black to take in heat, and underneath this is a thick layer of fat to keep them warm. Well adapted to their cold home, numbers of polar bears are dropping as global warming changes their environment. There are 20,000–25,000 in the wild, but experts think they could become extinct in the next 100 years if **climate change** continues.

SAVING WILDLIFE

Polar Bear

WWF (see page 28) is one of the leading groups involved in polar bear **conservation**. It researches how polar bears are being affected and works with governments and industries to reduce the impact of climate change. It also tries to prevent illegal **poaching** and trade in polar bears.

Since the 1970s, there has been an international agreement limiting hunting of polar bears, but now these animals face a greater danger—global warming.

A lone grizzly in the Arctic tundra

Brown Bears

Brown bears live within the Arctic Circle. In some parts of the U.S. and Canada, it is legal to kill grizzly bears (a type of brown bear) for sport even though they are endangered. In other areas, grizzlies are protected by the **Endangered Species Act**.

Another type of brown bear, the Kodiak bear, can only be found on the Kodiak Islands in Alaska. Although they are not threatened at present, the Alaska Department of Fish and Game helps monitor the bear population and preserves its habitat.

EXTREME ANIMALS

The Kodiak bear is the world's largest meat-eating land **mammal**, weighing up to 1,720 lbs. (780 kg).

Arctic Dogs

From small Arctic foxes to great gray wolves, wild dogs have adapted to life in the cold polar regions.

▲ *Gray wolves now roam freely in northern regions, but they are still hunted for their fur.*

Wolves in the Wild

Wolves have always been hunted by humans—for their fur or just out of fear. In 1984, the IUCN predicted that gray wolves might become extinct unless steps were taken to protect them. Today, they are no longer considered endangered, and although they are protected in some areas, in others, wolf hunting is still allowed.

WHAT DO YOU THINK?

Animals such as wolves prey on more endangered Arctic animals. How can we achieve a balance between protecting animals from **predators** without threatening the long-term survival of the wolves themselves?

SAVING WILDLIFE

Arctic Fox

Arctic foxes eat the food that polar bears leave behind. As there are fewer bears, the foxes are having trouble finding food. Arctic foxes are also being killed by red foxes, which have moved north as it gets warmer. In 2003, a European program called SEFALO was set up to monitor the foxes, provide food for them, and **cull** red foxes. Numbers rose in some areas as a result.

This Arctic fox is on the trail of food left behind by a polar bear.

Arctic Wolves

Arctic wolves, a type of gray wolf, are among the most fearsome polar predators. They can kill even big animals such as musk oxen (see page 13), but they can also go for weeks without food. Because Arctic wolves live in the most remote parts of the planet, they are not threatened by humans. But as climate change affects other animals, Arctic wolves are losing their traditional food supplies.

Arctic wolves live so far north that they are not often caught by humans.

Hoofed Animals

Many herds of hoofed animals make long journeys every year to and from the polar regions, but there are some that live in the freezing north all year round, including musk oxen, moose, and caribou.

▲ *Large herds of caribou (reindeer) live in the Arctic regions of Canada, Alaska, and Greenland.*

EXTREME ANIMALS

The antlers of the male caribou, found in far northern regions, can measure up to 5.9 ft. (1.8 m) from end to end.

5.9 ft. (1.8 m)

SAVING WILDLIFE

Musk Ox

At the beginning of the twentieth century, musk oxen were nearly extinct. In 1917, a law was passed that banned ox hunting and this saved them from dying out. The Wildlife Conservation Society has now launched a program to study how climate change is affecting the 80,000 Arctic musk oxen so they can prepare for this new threat.

▲ *There were no musk oxen left in Alaska at the start of the twentieth century. Now, populations are thriving.*

Caribou

One type of caribou—the Peary caribou—is endangered. The Inuit people have always hunted them for food, but now the deer population is declining because of oil exploration and global warming. Fifty years ago there were around 40,000, but now there are only 700 left. The Canadian government is working with local people to develop a conservation plan.

Dall Sheep

Agile Dall sheep live mainly in the Arctic National Wildlife **Refuge**, using its rocky landscape to flee from predators such as wolves and bears. Despite these natural dangers, the sheep are not yet under threat. If oil exploration is allowed in the refuge, though, that situation might change.

▶ *In the cold winter, Dall sheep will feed on frozen grass.*

Small Mammals

Small mammals such as marmots, voles, lemmings, squirrels, and hares all make their homes in the tundra and taiga, feeding on leaves and berries and making burrows beneath the snow.

Lemmings

Lemmings are one of the few creatures that live in the Arctic tundra all year round. In fact, they need the snow to make their burrows, and they rely on the ice to store their food. As climate change takes effect, lemmings might not be able to adapt to the warmer conditions.

▼ *Lemmings are a food source for many larger creatures, which may also be affected if numbers of lemmings drop.*

SAVING WILDLIFE

Wolverine

Ferocious wolverines are considered near threatened because of hunting. However, because populations are healthier in the icy northern regions, they are not a **protected species**, and people are still allowed to trap wolverines in Alaska. Environmental groups are trying to convince the authorities to make wolverines an endangered species so they will be protected by law.

Wolverines are known to be extremely vicious and can kill creatures much bigger than they are.

White Hares

Arctic and Alaskan hares often live in groups, huddling together for warmth. Their fur is white, so they are **camouflaged** against the snow. This protects them from natural predators such as wolves and human hunters and has helped keep them off the endangered list.

EXTREME ANIMALS

The Arctic ground squirrel is the only mammal that can make its body temperature drop below freezing. This stops it from using valuable fat stores and allows it to survive during **hibernation**.

Aquatic Animals

Marine mammals such as seals, walruses, and sea lions swim in the polar seas, but they also spend time on the ice, particularly when breeding. Global warming is thinning the sea ice and putting these animals at risk.

Saving Seals

Seals such as hooded seals, leopard seals, and elephant seals live in both the Arctic and Antarctic. Their greatest threat for many years has been hunting. The hunters say that there are plenty of some types of seal and that seal hunting is a traditional way of life for native people. **Conservationists** argue that seal hunting is cruel and unnecessary and that it should be banned.

▼ *The only natural predators of young leopard seals are killer whales (orcas) and some sharks.*

SAVING WILDLIFE

Hooded Seal

Although trade in hooded seals is banned in Canada and the European Union (EU), they are still hunted and traded illegally. Groups including the Seal Conservation Society and the Polar Conservation Organization are trying to prevent this practice. These groups also monitor the effects of climate change on the seal population.

▲ *Male hooded seals have a bulge on their forehead and nose, which they can blow up like a balloon to attract a mate.*

Hardy Walruses

Walruses spend most of their time in the water, diving for shellfish, but they come out on the ice to rest and to give birth, pulling themselves out of the water using their strong tusks. Walruses were once threatened by overhunting, but laws banning hunting mean that walrus numbers are on the rise again.

▼ *An Inuit hunter drags his seal kill along the ice.*

WHAT DO YOU THINK?

Some seals are only allowed to be hunted by local people using traditional weapons. Is it fair to say that some people can hunt them but not others? Why do you think hunters are only allowed to use traditional weapons?

Minibeasts

While insects are the most numerous creatures almost everywhere on earth, polar conditions make it hard for insects to survive. Despite this, a few hardy types of flies, mosquitoes, moths, and bees buzz around the cold poles.

It is not all ice in the Arctic landscape. Bees help ***pollinate*** *the flowers in the tundra region.*

EXTREME ANIMALS

The largest land **invertebrate** that lives in Antarctica all year round is a tiny insect called a midge!

A swarm of mosquitoes surrounds a Pacific loon on its nest in the Arctic National Wildlife Refuge.

Insects of the Air

Arctic bumblebees are important to the polar **ecosystem**. There are few plants and flowers here and they grow far apart, so the bees play a vital part in pollinating the flowers, which helps new ones to grow. Like other creatures, insects such as bees are affected by temperature changes in their environment. Conservation efforts to preserve polar habitats will help these important insects survive.

An Adaptable Arachnid

Arachnids are eight-legged creatures such as spiders and scorpions. One amazing spider has adapted to the changes in its polar environment caused by global warming. Studies over a period of ten years have shown that the Arctic wolf spider has grown a thicker **exoskeleton**—a skeleton on the outside of the body—that stops its body from drying out as its habitat heats up.

Penguin Paradise

There are 17 species of penguin around the world, but only four of them breed in Antarctica—Adélie, emperor, chinstrap, and gentoo penguins.

At Home on the Ice

Penguins have adapted to their icy habitat in a number of ways. Their feathers are short and tightly packed, and they have a thick layer of fat that extends right down their legs to protect them from the cold. They don't move easily on land, but they can move quickly through the water.

WHAT DO YOU THINK?

In 2007, the cruise ship *Explorer* sank close to Antarctica, spilling oil that endangered thousands of penguins and other marine animals. What are the benefits of polar cruises, and do you think they outweigh the dangers posed to the animals?

Baby emperor penguins protect themselves from the ice by standing on their parents' feet and snuggling into their feathers.

SAVING WILDLIFE

Gentoo Penguin

While more remote gentoo **colonies** are thriving, those that are closer to human settlements have been affected by human activity and pollution. Gentoos are now being bred in protected areas. Colonies are also being monitored to ensure no long-term damage is caused.

Far out on the sea ice, gentoo penguin colonies thrive.

Life in the Southern Ocean has its risks for penguins. They are eaten by seals.

Penguin Threats

Penguins' natural predators include seals, killer whales, and some sea birds. Most Antarctic penguins are not listed as endangered by international organizations, but **commercial** fishing and oil spills have both affected penguins. Like many polar animals, experts are also afraid of the effects global warming might have on polar penguin populations.

Polar Birds

Many sea birds, including guillemots, puffins, petrels, and albatrosses, spend the summer months at the poles and journey to warmer regions in the winter. They nest on the land but fetch their food from the polar oceans.

Hunters on Land and Water

Gyrfalcons are among the best hunters in the polar regions. They fly high above the Arctic tundra, searching for small animal prey on the ground below. Other birds, such as puffins, get their food from the cold waters. As numbers of small mammals and fish drop—due to climate change or habitat loss—the birds have to look elsewhere for their food.

▼ *Colonies of puffins nest along the coast of the North Atlantic and Arctic Oceans.*

Blending In

Many Arctic birds, such as the snowy owl, are almost completely white to help them blend in with their surroundings. Others, such as the ptarmigan—which stays in the Arctic all year round—have feathers that change color depending on the season.

Snowy owls can hardly be seen as they swoop across the snowy landscape.

EXTREME ANIMALS

Arctic terns **migrate** from the Arctic to the Antarctic and back every year. In a lifetime, this can add up to the same distance as going to the moon and back.

SAVING WILDLIFE

Peregrine Falcon

Peregrine falcons—which breed in the Arctic—nearly died out in the 1970s because of the use of a **pesticide** called DDT, which poisoned the insects eaten by the falcons. They were saved by **captive-breeding** programs and are now off the endangered list, although the effects of climate change on their Arctic populations are being watched carefully.

Some peregrine falcons breed in the Arctic tundra and fly south in the winter.

Whales in the Polar Waters

Whales such as the bowhead, beluga, and narwhal live in the polar seas all year round, while other species only spend part of the year in these icy waters.

Giants of the Deep

Whales of the Southern Ocean include fin whales, humpbacks, minke, and southern right whales. All these Antarctic whales migrate long distances every year, feeding in the polar seas during the summer months and heading to the warmer waters in the north to breed in the winter. Killer whales are also found in both Arctic and Antarctic waters, where special **sanctuaries** have been set up to protect their feeding grounds.

▼ *Humpback whales are found around the Antarctic coastline in the summer, but they breed in warmer waters.*

SAVING WILDLIFE

Antarctic Fin Whale

Fin whales were traditionally hunted for their meat, oil, and **baleen** (whalebone). By the 1970s, they had almost died out. The International Whaling Commission introduced laws to protect the fin whale in 1976, and since then, they have experienced a remarkable recovery. Their population is now estimated at around 120,000.

Despite coming close to extinction in the 1970s, there are now healthy populations of fin whales.

WHAT DO YOU THINK?

Should indigenous people be allowed to continue hunting whales if it is part of their culture, or should all whaling be banned for all people?

Save the Whale

Several species of Antarctic whale almost died out through hunting in the nineteenth century, but since then, international laws against whaling have helped them recover. However, hunting is still the biggest threat to these big sea mammals because countries including Japan and Norway refuse to stop, claiming they hunt the whales for research.

Organizations such as Greenpeace follow whaling boats to protest against the practice.

Fish and Other Sea Life

The polar oceans abound with life, and the creatures that live in the water are essential to the survival of all polar animals.

The Polar Web of Life

The Arctic food chain begins in the waters of the Arctic Ocean. Every polar creature depends on phytoplankton —microscopic plant forms that drift on the surface of the water. They convert energy from the sun into food and are then eaten by animal plankton, which in turn are eaten by other polar animals.

Life in the polar regions begins in the sea. Without fish, most other polar animals would struggle to survive.

Antarctic Invasion

As global warming causes water temperatures to rise in the sea around Antarctica, fish and other creatures such as crabs—which were previously unable to survive in the icy waters—are moving in. This is threatening the creatures that are already there. Some are preyed on by the invaders and others eat the food existing sea life depends on. Some of these fish are targets of commercial fishermen, who follow them into the polar waters.

Fishing in polar waters is threatening the survival of many species. A lot of research is needed to help in their conservation.

SAVING WILDLIFE

Patagonian Toothfish

In the 1990s, the Patagonian toothfish became a delicacy in restaurants. It was even named "Dish of the Year" in 2001 by a food magazine. It was so popular that fishermen rushed to catch it—and now it is critically endangered. Some countries limit the number that can be caught legally, and fishing is monitored by the Convention on the Conservation of Antarctic Marine Living Resources (CCAMLR), but it is still fished illegally.

EXTREME ANIMALS

The Antarctic ice fish has a special antifreeze chemical in its body, which stops it from freezing solid in the icy waters.

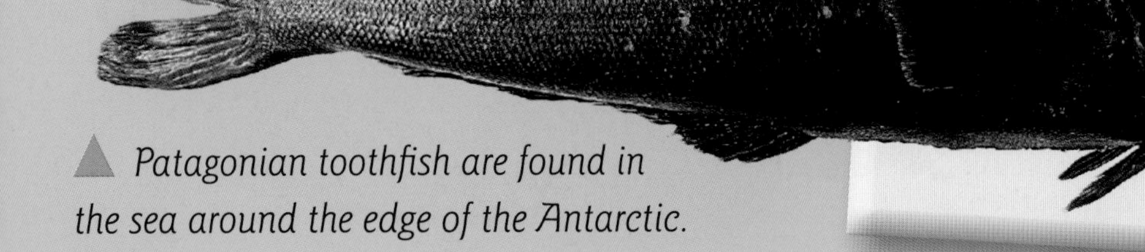

Patagonian toothfish are found in the sea around the edge of the Antarctic.

What Can We Do?

The biggest threat to polar animals is climate change, and this is something everyone can help reduce. Other threats, such as hunting, fishing, and habitat loss, are controlled by international organizations and national governments, but we can all play a part in saving polar animals.

Find out More...

Many organizations work to conserve polar species in different ways. Some of them focus on specific animals, and others campaign more generally to protect polar habitats as a whole.

WWF *(www.worldwildlife.org)*
This is the United States's site of the largest international animal conservation organization. On this site, you can follow links to information on all sorts of endangered animals and find out what WWF is doing to save polar creatures.

EDGE of Existence (www.edgeofexistence.org)
The EDGE of Existence is a special global conservation program that focuses on saving what it calls "Evolutionary Distinct and Globally Endangered" (EDGE) species—unusual animals and plants that are under threat.

International Union for Conservation of Nature (www.iucn.org)
The IUCN produces the Red List, which lists all the world's known endangered species and classifies them by how under threat they are, from least concern to extinct. You can see the whole list of endangered animals on the web site, as well as discover what the IUCN does to address environmental issues all over the world.

Convention on International Trade in Endangered Species (www.cites.org)
CITES is an international agreement between governments that aims to ensure trade in wild animal species does not threaten their survival. It lists animals that are under threat from international trading and makes laws accordingly.

Do More...

Tackle Global Warming

The greatest threat to polar animals is global warming, and everyone can help reduce it. Saving energy by turning off lights, computers, and other electrical appliances and limiting the use of fuels such as oil by walking or cycling rather than traveling by car can all help.

Sign a Petition

Petitions are documents asking governments or organizations to take action on something people are concerned about. Some of the organizations opposite have online petitions that you can sign to show your support for their campaigns.

Adopt an Animal

For a small contribution to some conservation organizations, you get to "adopt" a polar animal such as a polar bear or a penguin. They will send you information about your adopted animal and keep you up to date on all the conservation efforts in the area in which it lives.

Spread the Word

Find out as much as you can about the threats to polar animals and what people are doing to save them, and then tell your friends and family. The more support conservation organizations have, the more they can do!

Read More...

Polar Creatures
Wild Creatures
by Benita Sen
(PowerKids Press, 2008)

Polar Regions
Caring for the Planet
by Neil Champion
(Smart Apple Media, 2007)

Polar Regions
Earth's Final Frontiers
by Jim Kerr
(Heinemann Library, 2008)

The Polar Regions' Most Amazing Animals
Animal Top Tens
by Anita Ganeri
(Raintree, 2008)

Polar Animals Quiz

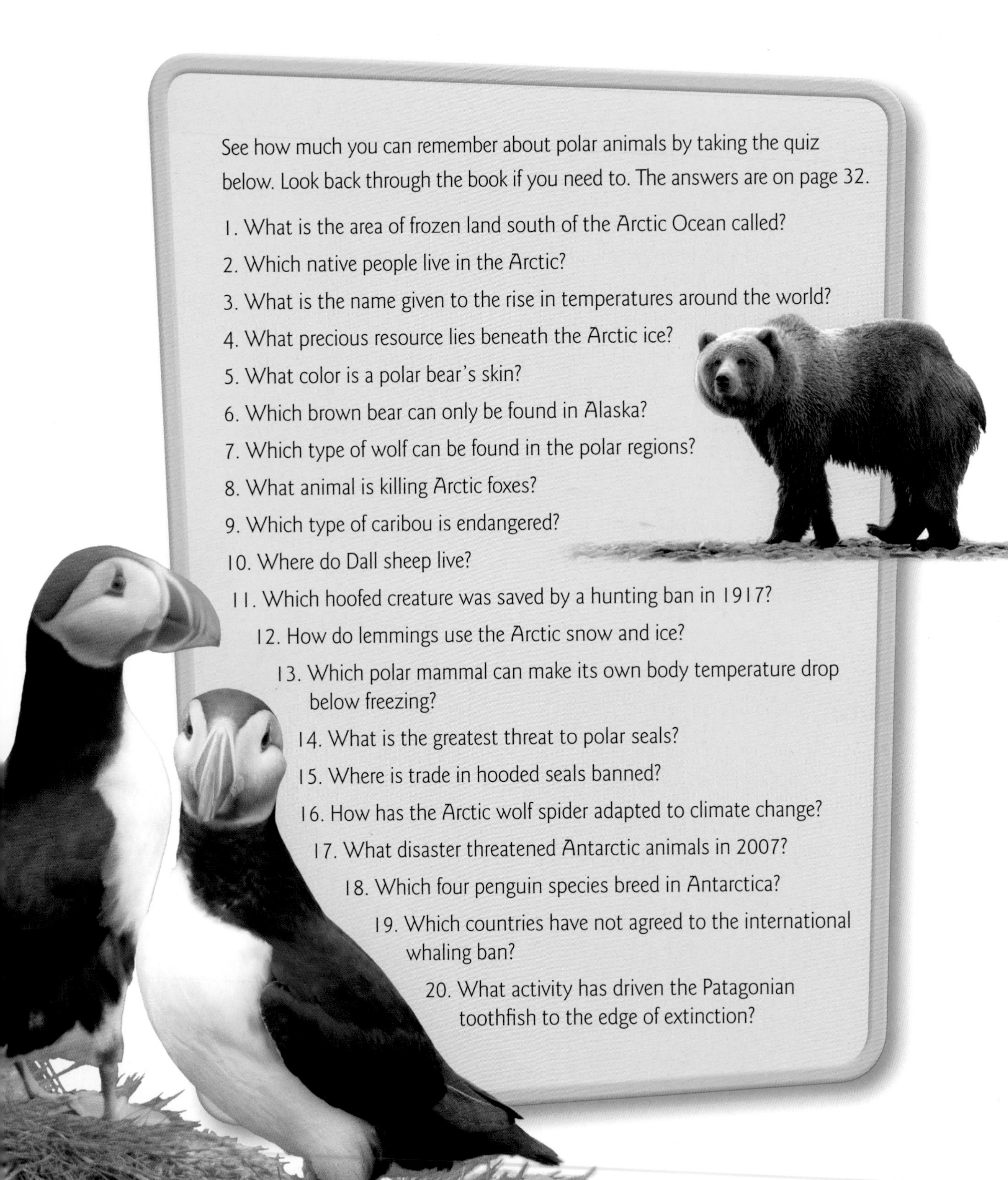

See how much you can remember about polar animals by taking the quiz below. Look back through the book if you need to. The answers are on page 32.

1. What is the area of frozen land south of the Arctic Ocean called?
2. Which native people live in the Arctic?
3. What is the name given to the rise in temperatures around the world?
4. What precious resource lies beneath the Arctic ice?
5. What color is a polar bear's skin?
6. Which brown bear can only be found in Alaska?
7. Which type of wolf can be found in the polar regions?
8. What animal is killing Arctic foxes?
9. Which type of caribou is endangered?
10. Where do Dall sheep live?
11. Which hoofed creature was saved by a hunting ban in 1917?
12. How do lemmings use the Arctic snow and ice?
13. Which polar mammal can make its own body temperature drop below freezing?
14. What is the greatest threat to polar seals?
15. Where is trade in hooded seals banned?
16. How has the Arctic wolf spider adapted to climate change?
17. What disaster threatened Antarctic animals in 2007?
18. Which four penguin species breed in Antarctica?
19. Which countries have not agreed to the international whaling ban?
20. What activity has driven the Patagonian toothfish to the edge of extinction?

Glossary

adapted changed in order to survive in new conditions
baleen a bony material found in the upper jaws of whales
camouflaged the color or patterns on an animal that help it blend in with its surroundings
captive breeding when endangered animals are specially bred in zoos or wildlife reserves so that they can then be released back into the wild
climate change a difference in the expected weather conditions or temperatures across the world
colonies groups of animals that live and work together
commercial something that is done to make money
conservation efforts to preserve or manage habitats when they are under threat or have been damaged
conservationists people who work to protect the natural environment
continent one of the earth's seven great landmasses—Africa, Antarctica, Asia, Australia, Europe, North America, and South America
cull when humans deliberately kill animals to keep their numbers down
ecosystem all the different types of plants and animals that live in a particular area together with the non-living parts of the environment
endangered at risk of becoming extinct
Endangered Species Act a law passed in America in 1973 to protect animals under threat of extinction by active conservation
exoskeleton a skeleton or shell outside the body
extinct when an entire species of animal dies out so that there are none left on earth
food chain a community of plants and animals in which each is eaten by another animal.
global warming the rise in average temperatures around the world as a result of human activity
habitat the place where an animal lives
hibernation when animals sleep or move around very little to survive during the winter
Inuit native people of the Arctic regions; sometimes called Eskimos
invertebrate an animal that doesn't have a backbone, such as an earthworm
mammal a warm-blooded animal that usually gives birth to live young
migrate to move from one place to another; many animals spend the summer in the Northern Hemisphere but migrate south when the weather gets colder.
native a person or animal that originates or occurs naturally in a particular country or region
pesticide a chemical often used by farmers to keep insects off their crops
poaching hunting an animal when it is against the law to do so
pollinate to transfer pollen from one flower plant to another so that it can make seeds and grow into a new plant
pollution spoiling the environment with man-made waste
predators animals that hunt others for food
protected species animals that are protected by law from hunting, trading, or other human activities
refuge a special area of land set aside for the protection of wildlife
resource something that people can use, such as oil or coal
sanctuaries special places where animals are protected or cared for if they are ill or injured
species a type of animal or plant
taiga a forested area south of the Arctic tundra
tundra a huge, permanently frozen, treeless plain just south of the Arctic Ocean

Index

Numbers in **bold** indicate pictures

Quiz answers

1. Tundra; 2. Inuit; 3. Global warming; 4. Oil; 5. Black; 6. Kodiak bear; 7. Arctic wolf; 8. Red fox; 9. Peary caribou; 10. Arctic National Wildlife Refuge; 11. Musk ox; 12. They burrow in the snow and store food in the ice; 13. Arctic ground squirrel; 14. Hunting; 15. Canada and the European Union; 16. It has grown a thicker exoskeleton; 17. An oil spill from the cruise ship *Explorer*; 18. Gentoo, Adélie, emperor, and chinstrap; 19. Norway and Japan; 20. Overfishing.